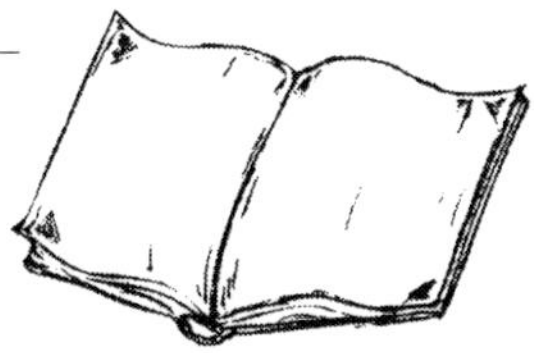

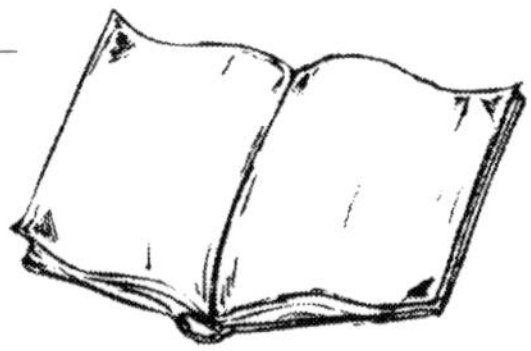

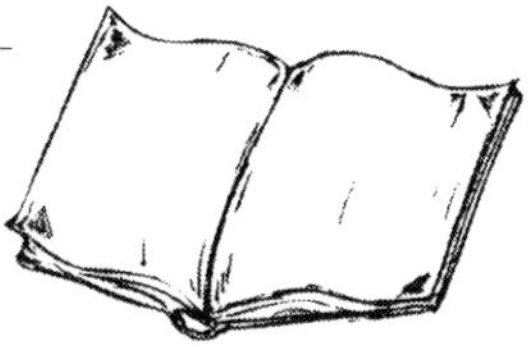

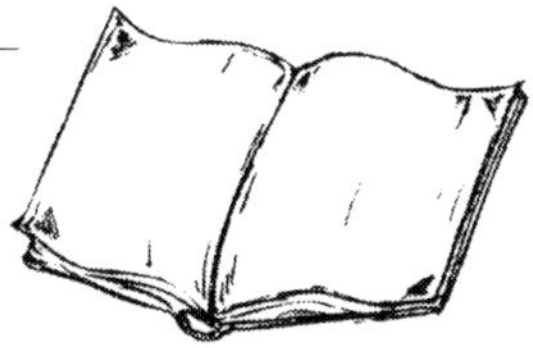

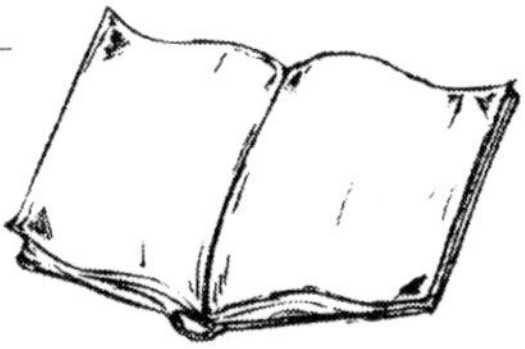

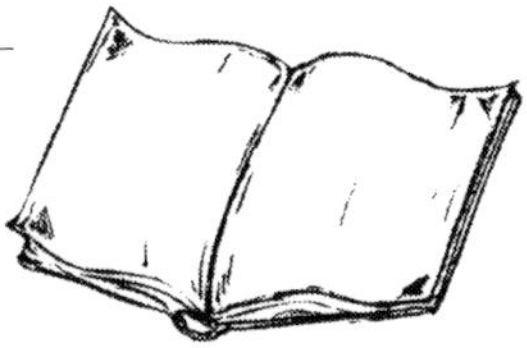

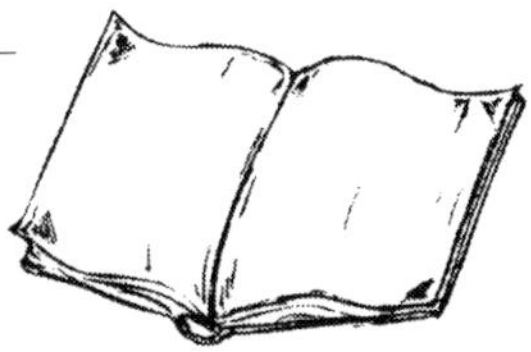

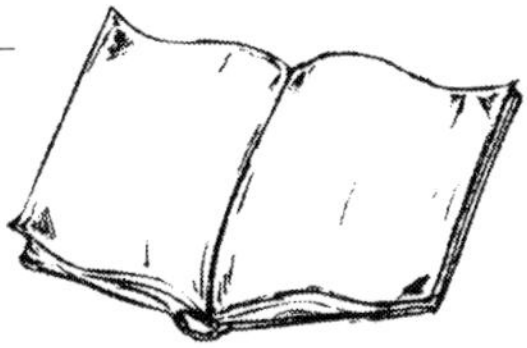

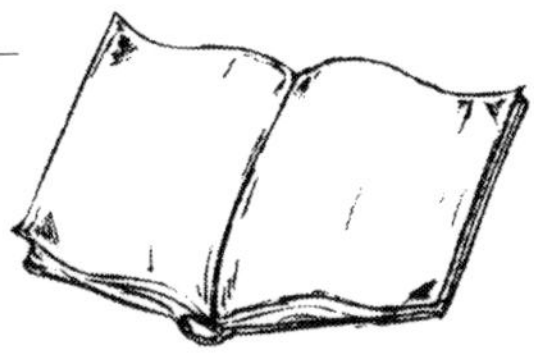

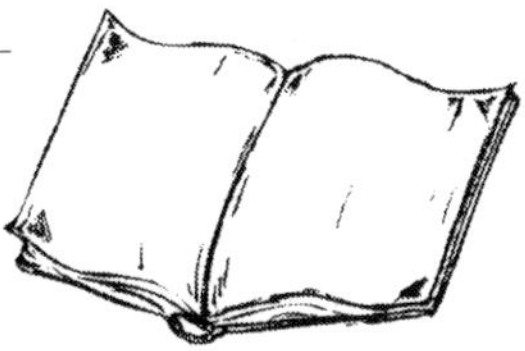

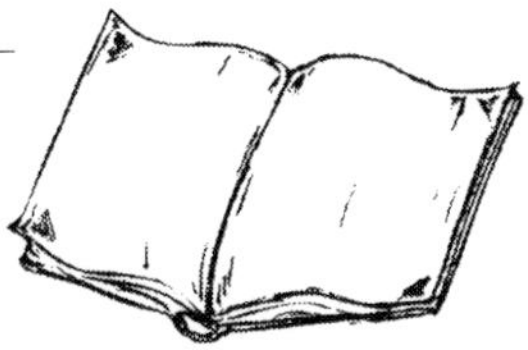

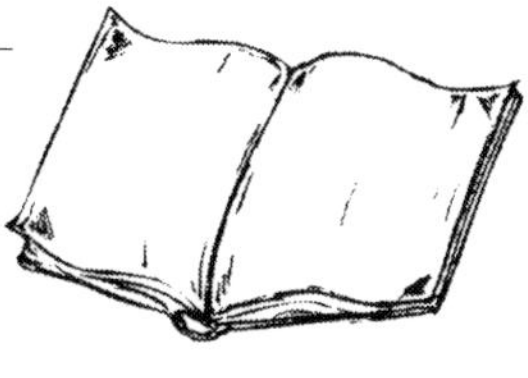

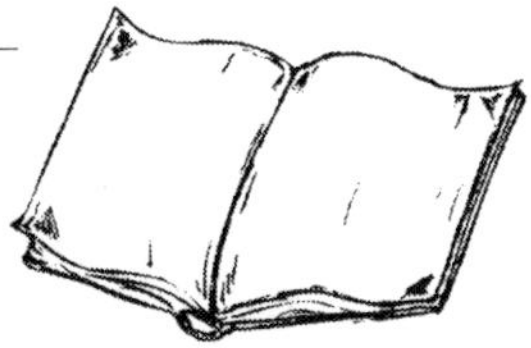

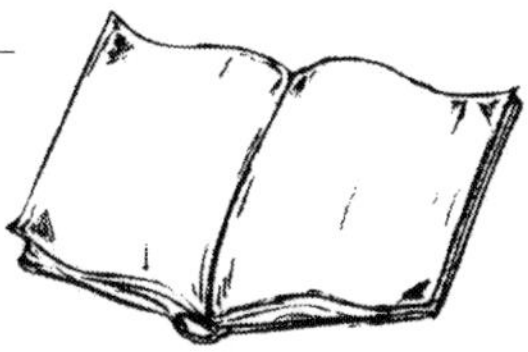

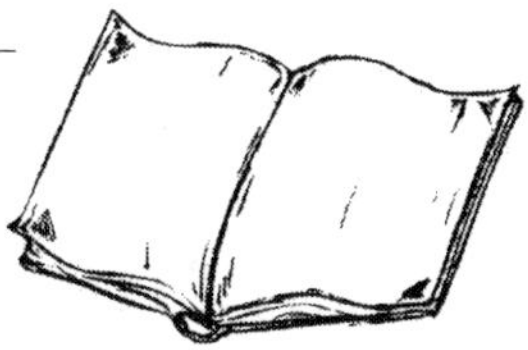

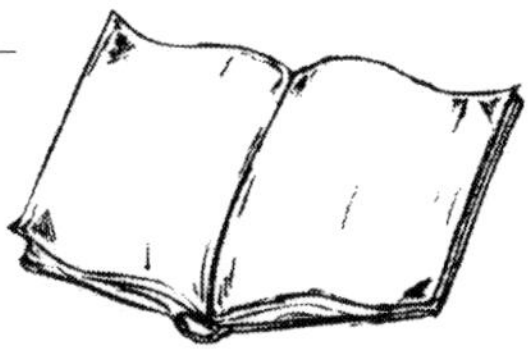

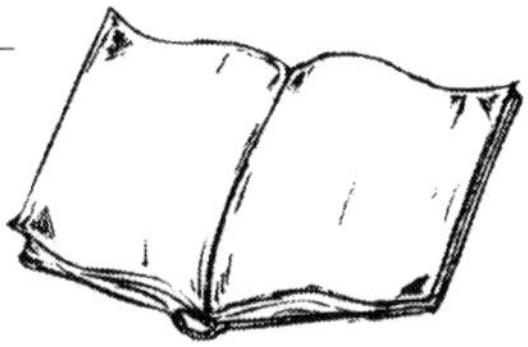

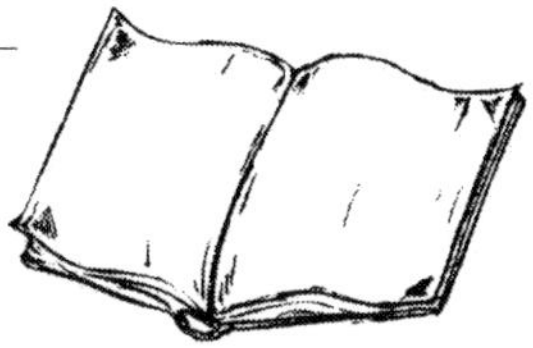

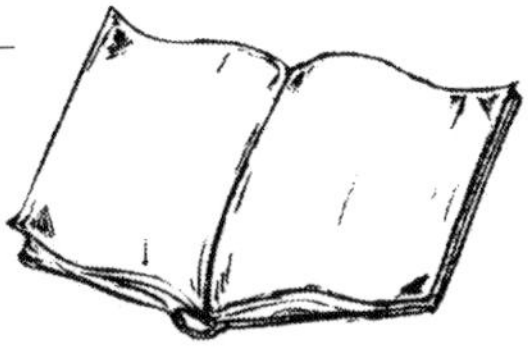

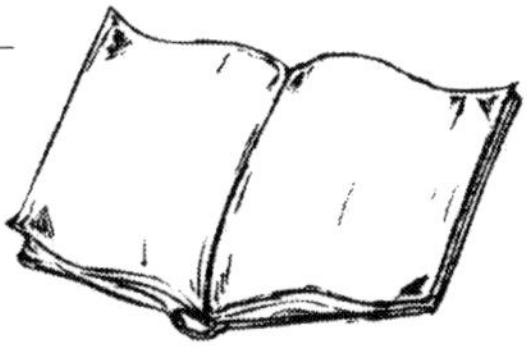

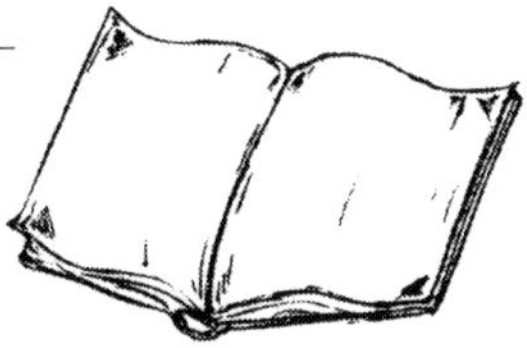

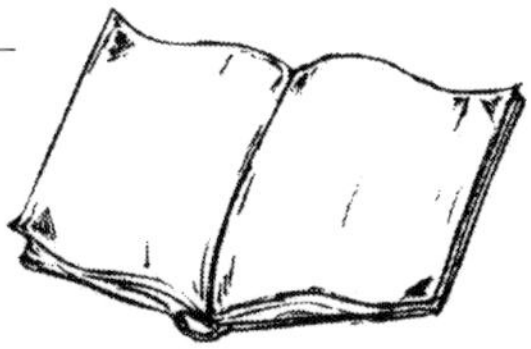

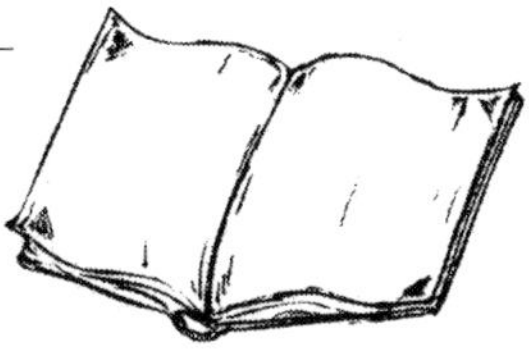

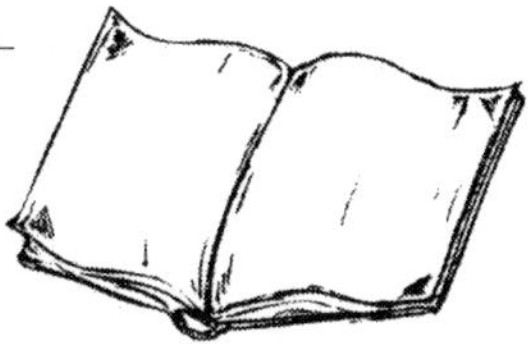

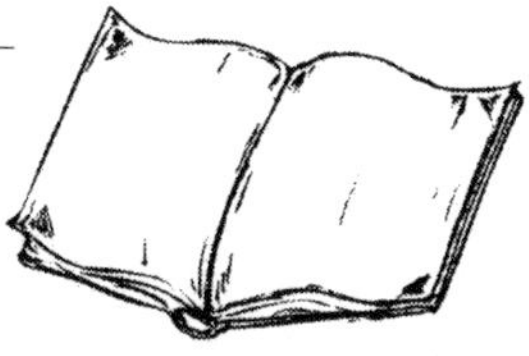

75703965R00084

Made in the USA
Columbia, SC
25 August 2017